PASSION FOR POETRY

PASSION FOR POETRY

Martin J. Rommel

To order additional copies of this book, contact:
Xlibris LLC
1-888-795-4274
www.Xlibris.com
Orders@Xlibris.com
142305

CONTENTS

THIS BOOK IS DEDICATED TO MY WIFE, RENEE MARIE WHO INSPIRED ME TO PUT MY THOUGHTS ON PAPER. THANKS FOR HELPING ME PUT THIS BOOK TOGETHER.

I WOULD ALSO LIKE TO POINT OUT SPECIAL POEMS WRITTEN. THE FIRST IS, *REUNITED*, IN MEMORY OF MY PETS JULIUS, TERIAKI GEM, AND BABY KING. FOR MY MOTHER-IN-LAW, CONSUELO MORALES, *A KEY TO HEAVEN*. *A NEW LIFE*, WRITTEN ESPECIALLY FOR OUR NIECE ALEXANDRIA MEADON. NEXT IS, *CAMBRIE ISABELLA*, SHE'S OUR NEXT GRANDCHILD, WHAT A GIFT OF LOVE FOR ALL TO BEHOLD. TO MY FATHER-IN-LAW, LEONARD OVIEDO. I LOOK TO HIM FOR INSPIRATION AS HE REPRESENTS THE PAST GENERATION. THANK YOU FOR ALL THE GREAT MEMORIES.

About The Author

MARTIN J. ROMMEL IS A NATIVE OF
LOUISVILLE, KENTUCKY RETIRED FROM
THE US NAVY THIS BOOK TOOK 3 YEAR TO
COMPLETE. HE CURRENTLY LIVES WITH
HIS WIFE, DOG, IN CAMPBELLSBURG, KY.
HIS HOBBIES ARE REFINISHING OLD
FURNITURE, AND STILL WRITES
POETRY. ENJOYS GOING TO FLEA MARKETS
AND AUCTIONS

Reunited

AS I LOOK INTO HEAVEN ABOVE
MY HEART GOES OUT TO THEE.
MY SOUL CRIES OUT FOR YOUR
RETURN. WITH THE WIND AT MY
BACK. AS THE RAIN DROP FALL
ABOVE I SEE THE LIGHT OF DAY A
RAINBOW. THERE NOT A DAY THAT
GO BY THAT YOUR NOT IN MY
PRAYER. YOUR SPIRIT LIVES ON
IN MY HEART FOREVER FOR ONE
DAY WE WILL BE REUNITED

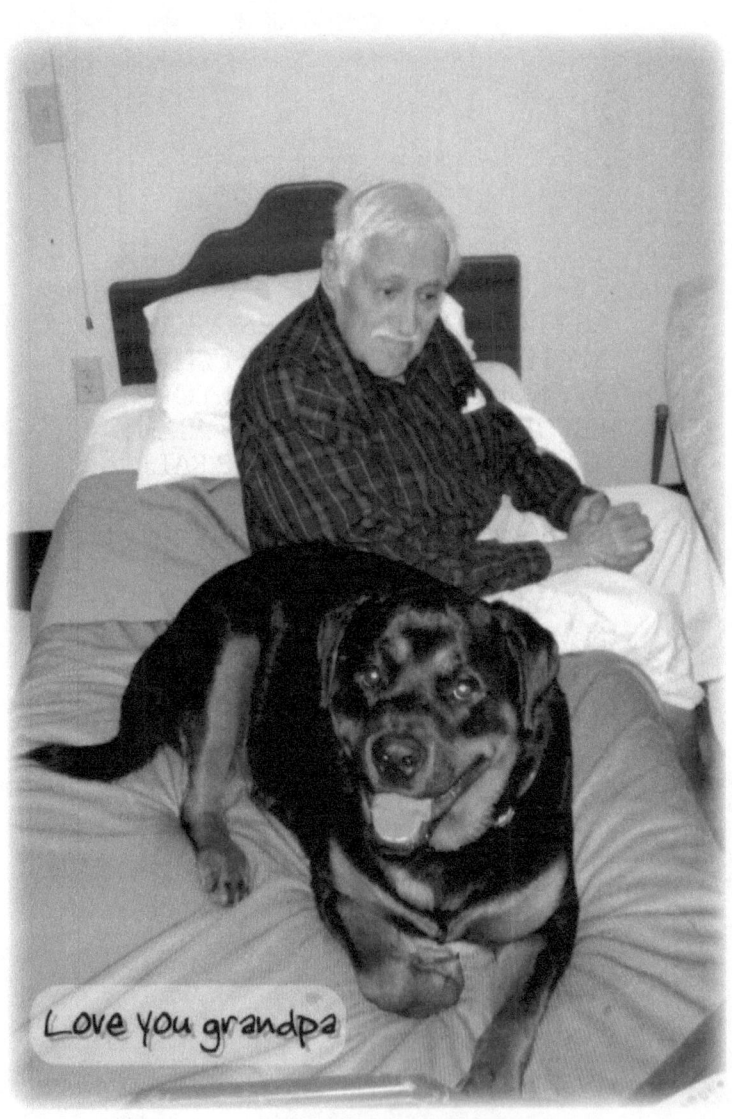

Love you grandpa

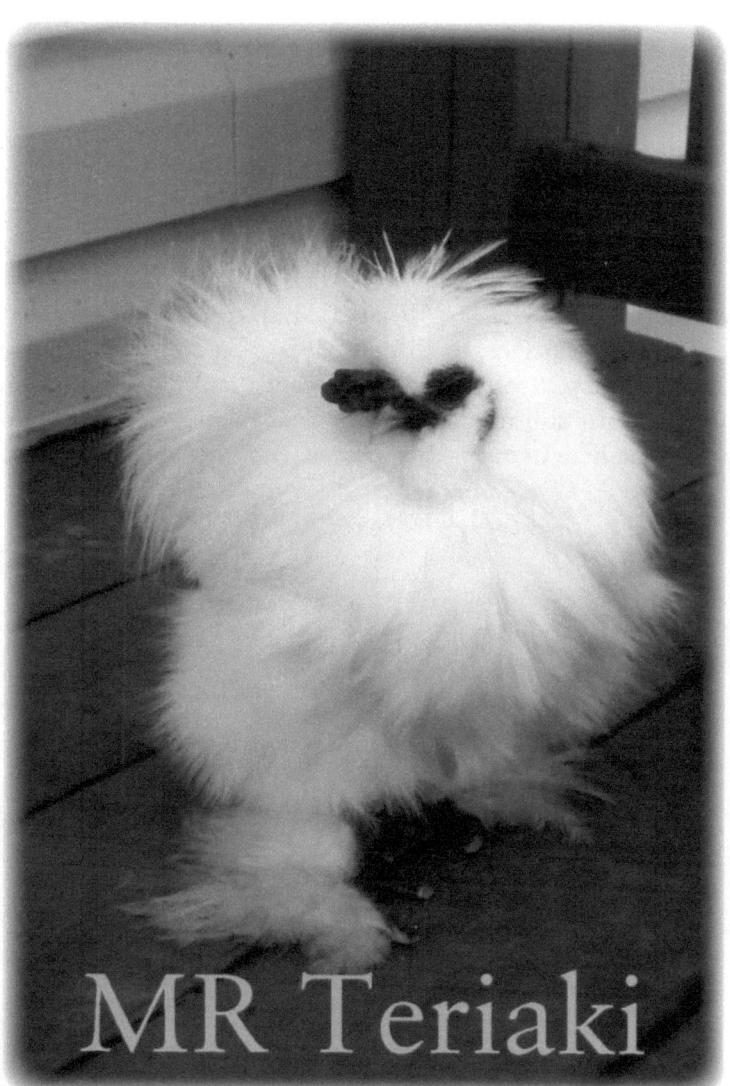

MR Teriaki

BABY KING

Baby King I miss you so. What a loyal companion you have been. From the smile on your face, to all that cheese you ate. Baby King you are a wonderful, loving dog. I so enjoyed our time we had together. I know in my heart that your spirit still resides with us. Your memories won't be forgotten, Baby King. You're here in our hearts forever.

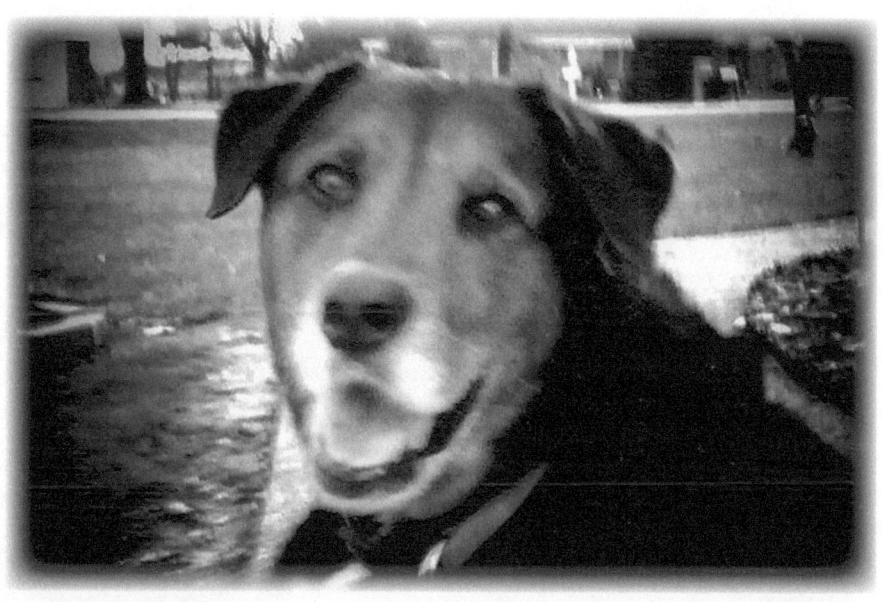

A Key To Heaven

A key to Heaven. As I pray one day that I can take that journey to a place like no other. Where all the soul meet. Where love is everlasting. No more hunger, no more pain. Home away from home. I must do my time here on earth so I can learn from others around me. My time is not at hand. One day I will get a key to heaven.

By
Martin J. Rommel

Written especially for my Mother-in-law Consuelo Morales

A NEW LIFE

A new life is at hand. The love you share is given in so many ways. You have your life's dreams close to your heart. Now is your time to shine with a new life. May the light of the world shine upon you with pride in all you do. Now time to move on, a new life for you. Like a rosebud so beautiful and yet so bold.

*Written especially for Alexandria Meabon,
My grand-niece for her college graduation.*

Martin J. Rommel

CAMBRIE ISABELLA

A gift of love for all to behold her beauty is like a rose so joyful in all her wisdom the raindrop above wash down upon her face like sun shine with pride. A journey to the sea that bring forth a life time of happiness Cambrie Isabella. You are special in my heart love grampa.

Autumn

Autumn's brilliant sound awaits us, as an eagle flies the blue skies above. A hawk flies into the distance for it's prey. A flock of butterflies flying gently into the wind. The leaves put on a show of spectacular color. Autumn. The time is now to endure in all it's glory.

EAGLE FLY

AS DAWN ENTERS INTO THE WIND SO AS EAGLE FLY FREE IN THE SPIRIT OF THE DAY. FOR OUR FOREFATHERS GATHER AROUND THE FIRE OF FREEDOM THE MIST OF THE MORNING BURNS OFF. DAWN TAKE OVER BRING FORTH NEW LIFE IN THIS WORLD THE EAGLE STAND FOR POWER THAT WE HAVE INSIDE OUR HEART. OUR FOREFATHERS GAVE UP THEIR LIVES SO WE CAN HAVE A BETTER WAY OF LIFE TODAY. FLY LIKE AN EAGLE LET YOUR HEART BE FREE

MAGICAL HEARTS

I LOVE YOU WITH ALL MY HEART GENTLE ROLLING HILLS SURROUND ME WITH YOUR LOVE RAIN DROPS FALL DOWN UPON ME CLEANSING MY HEART LIKE WILD FLOWERS RUNNING WILD INTO THE WIND THEIR MAGICAL WAYS. MY LOVE FOR YOU HOLD NO BOUNDARY. AS TIME SAILS AWAY MY LOVE CRIES OUT FOR YOU. A JOURNEY I TAKE OF A LIFE TIME OF JOY FOR ARE HEARTS ARE TOGETHER. KINDLE OF LOVE FOREVER.

DAYBREAK

A new dawn is at hand. As I look around the forest I see the deer foraging for food. The flowers bloom for a new day. The sun rises in the east and brings with it warmth to the earth and bright colors that surround us. To the birds flying above. Daybreak, as the sea washes upon the shoreline bringing with it a message in a bottle of mystic love.

CROSSROAD

Crossroads in the moonlight. As I make my way along the river's edge. From a distance, I see fish jumping and wild birds flying. See me now, for I'm at my crossroads in my life. My dreams have come true with the winds at my back, the glory of hope, I surrender my soul. Then I can make the journey home.

IMAGES

Images in the mirror, reflections of love in my heart. To follow one's dreams, look and it can be found in the mirror. Images of light dancing into the night. Behold the reflections of nature's beauty. Peace and happiness is at hand. For there is not a day that goes by that we don't look into the mirror for guidance and wisdom.

THE OCEAN

The ocean, what a sight to see. To the songs of the seagulls above flying in the midday, to the waves crashing along the shoreline. To the children running about the ocean front. Seeing people of all ages hand in hand walking along the waterfront. The ocean renews my soul. Gives me an inner peace that endures.

LOVED ONES

Loved ones, where have they gone? To a place out of reach. Their spirits live on. Within us, where have they gone? Their love is so true, pure as gold. So don't let your heart be troubled, for one day we will be with them in that place called heaven.

CELTIC JOURNEY

Celtic journey. Allow yourself to be transported to a magical place. Where the sweet and bittersweet sounds beckon you to become part of a wonderful fantasy. Celtic journey. Discover places you've only dream of, now coming alive within you. The winds that gently carry you along on this Celtic journey.

SUNSET ON THE SEA

Sunset on the sea, what a beautiful sight to behold! From the salt in the air, to the birds flying overhead, my eyes can see wave after wave washing up upon the bay. As the sunsets on the sea, I go back in time thinking about all the good times that we shared. For the love of the sea is everlasting. What beauty lays within my heart for you. Sunset on the sea.

Journey Home

My journey home has come. I must go now to seek out my own peace. Time for me to rest now. A long journey home. For love is everlasting. Be happy and joyful for me. Don't let your heart be troubled. My spirit is with thee now and forever.

THE SOUND OF MUSIC

The sound of music playing in my heart, essence of change is set free to the world around me. Free to explore the sounds of music as wings of a dove flies free. As the music plays, my spirit is set free to the world around me. For the love of music is like a waterfall washing over me. Cleansing my soul.

LOVE ME

Love me for who I am. I love thee with all my heart and soul. For I can look into your eyes and see the firing glow. Your smile lights up my day. Your beauty is like no other. The days grow shorter and the nights grow longer. For my love for thee I hold so true. Love me for who I am, for I love thee. Take my hand my love and walk with me.

HEAVEN

Look down from heaven above. For my soul to keep. As I look for thee in the garden, your footprints in the sand draw me closer to you. Our love has no boundaries, only memories of you, my dear. Dance with me in heaven where the sands of time endure the long journey home. My love, I will kiss you for the last time this very evening. For alone back to heaven I must go to teach others the way home.

Take Me Home

Take me home to the sea. Pick me up and put me in a seabag. Ship me off to a distant land. For this old salt the sea is calling home. For a lighthouse needs to be manned. So I ask you one more time, pick me up and put me in the seabag. Hurry now! I am tired and my time is short here on earth. So help out this old salt by taking me home to the sea.

WHAT IS LOVE?

What is love? Love is in most part thoughts and feelings we share in spirit and courage. One's inner most nature. Love is strong and affectionate for one another. Love is proud. Love is the greatest gift we have to share. So love that special someone in your life. Love is what you make of it.

MOUNTAIN TOP

As I look down from the mountain top, I hear the sounds of wildlife in the distance. The smell of wild flowers that fill the summer air around me. The sunshine as it lays down upon me. The mountain top is a place of splendor and peace. Live on in the hearts of all.

I Am One Of Many

I am one of many. I hold the tree of life in my hands. I am the giver of joy to the hearts that seek me out. I am the sounds of love in the distant night. I am one of many. As the sun rises and the water flows over a waterfall, and you can see a mountain top from afar. I am one of many parts of creation, look for me not, look in your heart you hold the key.

REFLECTIONS OF LOVE

Reflections of love are in the air. A gift of all seasons. As a river that flows into the sea and birds of all kinds flying the long distance home. Reflections of love are like the flowers that bloom in the spring. A rose that keeps on giving. Love is part of our lives, within our hearts and soul. Sounds of water flowing down a waterfall, to a wave that crashes along a shoreline. To know love is to be loved.

TEAR DROP

Tear drops of rain washing away the blood from my heart. Just to hold you. Let me be your true love. Tear drops of rain running down my face. Thunder in the night keeps me awake. Hold on now, don't run away. I'm here for you. I have tear drops of rain. I can see it in your eyes your love for me is there. You're all I need to keep me free from the tear drops of rain.

Embrace The Spirit

Embrace the spirit of the butterfly and accelerate your own transformation. Tap into the strength and wisdom of your own butterfly spirit. Go forward, be free! Into the wind let your soul be your guide home. So embrace the spirit of the butterfly.

Walk With Me

Walk with me my love. Give me your hand. We will travel a journey like no other. You have my soul to keep, my love to hold onto. To the sea we will go. Walk with me my love. As I look into your eyes I see the reflection of love you have for me. As the waves wash over the sands of time, our love will endure. Walk with me.

AUTUMN ROSE

Autumn rose I will always remember our love. Wind in the willow. All alone, we share our love at sunset on the sea cliff every time we meet there. Butterflies in the garden. Evening comes, take my hand please, stay awhile. I give thee an autumn rose as a gift of my love to thee.

THE LIGHT

The light is a gift of well being. An inner peace that I seek. The light so bright, but yet so warm to the touch. One day we all shall see the light and not live in darkness. In time we shall pass from this world to the next. Let the light be your guide. Open your heart, let yourself be free. Embrace the light that shines down from the heavens. Raindrops shall dance down from above washing away that once was, but now is renewed. The light the giver of light.

Meadows Of Dreams

Meadows of dreams are full of spring flowers that come to mind, when I'm away from thee. Journey across this land with me, hand in hand. My everlasting love I give to thee. My heart I give up to you to hold. A key to a dream is what life is made of. So dance with me in the meadows of dreams.

LET FREEDOM RING

Let freedom ring throughout this great land of ours. From the mountaintops above to the sea below. Let freedom ring. Be grateful for what you have. Open your hearts to others around you, share the freedom. For our forefathers and many other great people gave up so much for us to have the freedom we have today. Let tears of joy open your eyes to the freedoms we enjoy today. Let freedom ring.

POETRY

Poetry is a work of art. Elegant detail creating just the right words to say. Poetry is a garden of opportunity for all. The best of everything. Poetry is the reflection of love. Extraordinary measures for everyday wisdom from the heart.

ALL ALONE

All alone. Where do I go from here? Looking for that special place called home. I need someone to be with, to share my life with, to love one with all my heart and soul. All alone. Away from home. Can you be that person for me? The songs coming from the water help ease my pain. Find me please. I'm all alone. For one day, I will find that loved one. Then I won't be alone.

RUNNING WILD

Running wild into the wind, I was lost, now I am at home in the wild. Where the butterflies roam and the mustangs run wild. Where eagles fly high in the sky and fish that swim in the streams. Born to be free. I am part of all creation. I am the American Indian. Running wild into the wind.

SONGS OF LOVE

Songs of love spoken here. Like a rose so beautiful to look upon, but yet so fragile. Songs of love flow throughout my body. Sunshine sparkles in the water by the bay. My love for you I hold so true. Songs of love bring life to that which once was lost and now is found. Wondrous love like a dream of all dreams. Something to hold onto, like a rose in all it's beauty. Keep the songs of love in your heart forever.

QUIET

Quiet of the night. The moon is so bright. A sound of a train coming from afar breaks the quiet of the night. I look for peace in the night. My time to be free to dance on a mountain top, to dream, to rest my soul in the quiet of the night.

Summer Night

Heat of the day brings forth a summer night. Rain. A gust of wind picks up, then comes the rain to cool the earth down. The thunder and lightening put on a great show of force. Lightening dancing into the night sky. Rain clouds linger overhead. Then with a gust of wind, the rain moves forward into the night.

Time After Time

Time after time I wish you were here. I miss you so. I cherished the time we had together. I must let you take your journey home. My time to heal and move on. Time after time I too will be with thee. I wish you well my dear friend. Our love is as the sun, bright to one's eyes. So beautiful to behold.

Take My Hand

Take my hand, come with me. Let's be like two birds wild and free flying from tree to tree. Love birds. The sound of music we can make. Our hearts are one with the wind. Take my hand, let me show you the love that I can give you. The peace and happiness within you. Let yourself be free. Oh! Where have you gone? Come back to me. Take my hand, my love.

LIFE

Life's a challenge. Thoughts of tomorrow weigh on my mind. Trying to keep my distance from the sadness and pain. What a challenge my memories give to me. Good or bad, I find that everyday is a challenge. I will move forward. I must for my own sake. I look for other ways for dealing with life's challenges. In music, poetry, family, and friends life's a challenge for the young and old alike. So relax your mind and body, life goes on. Let yourself be free from life's challenges.